D1626666

This book is to be returned on or bef

IN OLD PHOTOGRAPHS

BRITAIN

IMAGES OF LOWESTOFT

THE PHOTOGRAPHS OF CHRISTOPHER WILSON

IAN G. ROBB

Sutton Publishing Limited
Phoenix Mill · Thrupp · Stroud
Gloucestershire · GL5 2BU

First published 2002

British Library Cataloguing in Publication Data
A catalogue record for this book is available from the
British Library.

ISBN 0-7509-2992-8

Typeset in 10.5/13.5 Photina.
Typesetting and origination by
Sutton Publishing Limited.
Printed and bound in England by
J.H. Haynes & Co. Ltd, Sparkford.

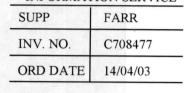

A member of the Lowestoft
Amateur Operatic & Dramatic
Society resplendent in his
costume as one of the cast of
Veronique at the Marina Theatre,
January 1923. A great favourite
with theatre-goers and amateur
theatricals alike, *Veronique* was
also well received by the
Lowestoft Journal of the time.

CONTENTS

Christopher Wilson, a self-portrait, *c.* 1939. Although born in Sleaford, he was quickly attracted to the charms of Lowestoft and to Oulton Broad in particular. After opening his own studio in the town in 1903, he rapidly established himself as one of Lowestoft's foremost photographers.

INTRODUCTION

When Christopher Wilson arrived in Lowestoft in 1893, the town had been a hive of activity for fifty years. One of the foremost resorts of the East Coast, yet to reach its peak as a prosperous fishing port, it was split between the old and the new towns. The latter was Sir Morton Peto's plan to turn Lowestoft into a superior watering place, and was visited by nobility, gentry and up-and-coming successful professionals alike. Peto had also turned Lowestoft into a thriving commercial port with a formidable fishing fleet. During the herring season, some 80 per cent of all fish caught was exported, turning the whole town into one huge fish-processing plant. Every year the harbour would be choked with vast numbers of English and Scottish drifters following the herring down the coast. The Fish Market itself was in the midst of expansion – the Waveney Market opened in 1883 to cope with the increase in fishing boats, and extensions to the Trawl Dock had only been completed in 1892, a year before Christopher's arrival.

Lowestoft, however, had a two-fold reputation – not only its fishing, but also its resort, where during the summer months, the town concentrated on the visitor, who in the beginning was here to take the waters, but before long came solely for relaxation. A small army of doctors, surgeons and dentists had also arrived, many making tidy fortunes tending to the needs and whims of the wealthy. Each summer Lowestoft transformed itself into one vast pleasure ground – hotels, parks, entertainments, promenades and the South Pier, all culminating with the Regatta in the last week of August – and all geared towards the visitor.

The railway was the lifeblood of the town, linking Lowestoft directly to London, the Midlands and the north. It delivered Lowestoft fish to almost every corner of the country and in return brought in its visitors, as well as those seeking opportunities in the rapidly growing town. In 1893 these included Christopher Wilson, a young photographic assistant from Lincolnshire, his new wife and their three friends.

Born in October 1872, in the small market town of Sleaford, Christopher was the youngest of the four children of Thomas and Phoebe Wilson, groom and housemaid in service at Carlton Scroop, the home of the Earl of Winchelsea. Sadly, the young Christopher was not to know his father for very long, being only two years old when Thomas died from the result of a riding accident. Now a widow, Phoebe continued in service for a while, periodically taking her young son with her to the big house. One of the Winchelsea family was an amateur photographer and it may have been here that Christopher, albeit a child, was introduced to his first camera. Phoebe never remarried, and at the age of ten Christopher joined the rest of the Wilson children in supporting their mother. Little else is known about his early life until 1888, when almost sixteen years old, he was apprenticed to Sleaford photographer, W. Starkey Downes. The apprenticeship lasted four years, in which time Christopher learnt his profession and also met his future wife, Agnes Watkinson, the daughter of the local miller. He received his indentures as a photographic assistant in 1892, a month before his twentieth birthday, and married Agnes in early 1893. Soon after, he began making plans for his future – plans that would bring him to the north-east corner of Suffolk, and to Lowestoft.

At the time of Christopher Wilson's arrival in the town, Lowestoft was going through one of its periodical phases of expansion, not only with new shops in London Road North, but developing new residential areas – the Brickfields around Norwich Road, the St Margaret's Road and Cambridge Road area, as well as continuous building in south Lowestoft.

All this activity brought not only the opportunist, those ready to set up business or who were looking for work, but also introduced the professional photographer as part of what would be known today as the town's service industry, despite the fact that there had been photographic studios in Lowestoft for nearly forty years.

From his arrival in 1893 to 1946, when he took his last photographs, Christopher Wilson's fortunes mirrored those of the town. The years up to 1914 saw him as a successful family man rising from an assistant to running his own studio. Not as prolific as his employer Boughton, he nevertheless contributed much to recording the life of the town. Throughout the First World War he, like other local photographers, also recorded the soldiers and sailors going off to fight, many never to return, as well as their wives, sweethearts and families. And, like Lowestoft, he suffered from the immediate postwar slump, but succeeded in keeping afloat in the Depression of the 1930s, which nearly crippled Lowestoft's fishing fleet.

The closest British town to Germany, Lowestoft was to suffer heavily from air attacks during the last war. Christopher's old studio, then leased to H.G. Hannant, was in the path of the devastation caused by the attack on the town centre in January 1942, to be ever remembered as the Waller raid, the worst on the town, and in which the studio received considerable damage.

Images of Lowestoft is a unique record of the town from 1894 to 1946, as seen by a man who was in an advantageous position to record some of the people and events that shaped Lowestoft in those auspicious years of the early twentieth century, and who, in his own small way, created history himself. Unless otherwise identified, all the photographs in this book were taken by Christopher Wilson. With the exception of those on pages 9 and 26, which are included to show the town as it was at two important points in his career, the remainder are from examples collected by Christopher or the Wilson family.

1

Lowestoft in the 1890s

Sorting the fish on one of Lowestoft's many smacks at the Waveney Dock, *c.* 1899. The town was then at its peak as a herring port. Because of short fishing trips and the railway, sea-fresh Lowestoft fish would arrive at the many inland markets within a day of landing.

The Royal Hotel standing proud over the South Beach and the Esplanade, *c.* 1890. Taken by an unidentified photographer, this image epitomises the town so favoured by those visiting mainly for pleasure. The donkey man, with his charges nearby, and the approaching deckchair attendant both ply for trade, passing among ladies and gentlemen dressed up to the nines. One had to be dressed properly – even if it meant wearing a suit on the beach!

LT 636 *Two Sisters* about to go through the pier-head, *c.* 1893. This was taken by an unnamed photographer looking from the South Pier. Fishing had been part of the town's tradition for centuries, but it was Peto's vision in linking it with the new resort and the railway that was responsible for the town's phenomenal growth in the later years of the nineteenth century.

London Road North, *c*. 1892. A view by Frith of Reigate taken a year before the young Christopher Wilson arrived in Lowestoft. This road was originally called South Street. The gardens on the left belonged to large detached houses and contrasted sharply with the new shops opposite. One building, however, stands out, and that is the single-storeyed castellated prefabricated photographic studio of John Barrett, originally constructed in 1863 for his father, Michael. On the opposite side the northern entrance to the Marina, then a crescent, lies between the Free Methodist church and W.T. Balls' auction rooms, then under construction and hidden behind hoardings. W. Clarke, watchmaker and jeweller, and Chamberlain's hairdressing rooms could be found among the shops near the camera, as could the recently opened studio of W. Boughton & Sons, one of the many businesses tempted into the town. Managed by Boughton's son Thomas, it was here that Christopher Wilson was employed as a photographic assistant, beginning his career in Lowestoft with the task of taking run-of-the-mill portraits. Before long, however, his employer discovered his flair for landscape – a boon in a town like Lowestoft. Christopher would stay with Boughton for nearly ten years, moving with them to 54 London Road North in 1894. The majority of Christopher Wilson's photographs in this chapter were taken for Boughton; only right at the end, in 1898, did he start to venture out on his own.

Wellington Terrace and Gardens, late 1890s. The terrace was named after Arthur Wellesley, Duke of Wellington, who died in 1852 just as it was being constructed. The scene here is of the peace and tranquillity of a summer morning outside Sir Morton Peto's centrepiece to his new resort. Victoria Terrace and Marine Parade were not as yet connected, and Wellington Terrace could only be reached from London Road South by way of Claremont Road or Wellington Road (now Waterloo Road). The trees between Victoria Terrace and the large house adjoining Wellington Gardens mark part of the Olympian Gardens and in particular the mews where the visiting gentry, down for the season and staying at the two terraces, would stable their horses and carriages. A young boy rides his horse along Wellington Esplanade, past a small German band, and following behind a one-horse open charabanc, converted for the season from an ordinary cart, offering rides to 'Park Pier and Kirkley' for *3d*. Needless to say, the ability of Christopher Wilson to produce views like this quickly made him a valuable asset to his employer. Today, unfortunately, the scene is not so peaceful. At present Wellington Terrace looks down on traffic thundering past its doors travelling towards Ipswich and London.

St John's church and rectory, *c.* 1894. The church was designed by John Louth Clemence and built in 1854. Unusually, this scene is almost a straight copy of one taken by Frith some years earlier – indeed, Wilson used the same vantage point. The rectory became a dentist's surgery in later years (a Mr Butcher was there in the 1930s) and still survives, although the church itself was demolished in the late 1970s.

The Harbour Hotel with St John's church and Pier Terrace, late 1890s. Almost everyone here seems to be travelling towards the bridge. Of particular note is the shoeshine 'boy' on the left, complete with customer in attendance. Although Holroyd appears as mine host on the hotel frontage, W. Crocker was running the Harbour Hotel by 1898.

The upper part of the High Street, *c.* 1896, photographed from opposite the Town Hall by Charles Metcalf not long before the west side of the street was demolished for road widening. By the mid-1890s this part of the town was described as nothing more than public houses and brothels. Certainly there were a considerable number of public houses near by; on the left, nearest to the camera, was the Anchor Brewery Stores on the corner of Mariner's Street. Adjoining it was the Town Hall, built on the site of the old Corn Cross and surrounded by yet more public houses. The shuttered Victoria House, however, was in fact J.B. Cooper, draper and milliner. Most of the premises opposite on the cliffside have survived. Arthur W. Smith, grocer and provision merchant, where the two young women and the girl with the pram are, was an old-established business dating back to the 1830s. The Wicks brothers were there in the 1860s; one was a butcher and the other a grocer. Smith had taken over by the 1880s and remained there for fifty years. Remembered as Johnny Belton's, the shop continued until the mid-1970s. Christopher Wilson himself had photographed the upper part of the High Street for Boughton about the same time as Metcalf; however, no pictures are known to have survived apart from a reproduction in *O'Driscoll's Annual* for 1899.

St Margaret's church by an unknown photographer, late 1890s. Half a mile from the town and reached then by a country lane, the present church dates from 1483. It is not known who the woman is, but the clerical gentleman coming towards her is believed to be the incumbent, the Rev. D.A. Lawrence.

Old cellar, High Street, c. 1897. This is possibly one of the earliest photographs of the medieval merchants' cellars which were discovered during the widening of the High Street. Dating from the mid-fifteenth century and possibly built by the same craftsmen who constructed St Margaret's, the cellars' similarity in style to the church has led many to believe in error that there was once a religious establishment on the site.

LT 634 *Sam J Dobson* and LT 10 *George Lake* about to be overtaken by the Yarmouth paddle tug *United Services*, 1898. Built in 1887, she was in her second year of pleasure trips from Yarmouth to London, stopping off at Lowestoft. Her success was soon followed by others, culminating with the Claremont Pier being built as a landing stage for the Belle steamers in 1903.

Ramsgate boats off to the fishing grounds on a less than ideal day, *c.* 1898. Lack of wind has meant that at least two of the vessels have to make their way by oars instead of sails. Moored at the South Pier is the *Caroline Hamilton*, about to take passengers on a short trip. A private lifeboat commissioned after the Great Gale of 1882, she was used mainly as a pleasure craft from 1893.

Lowestoft Harbour, looking towards Pier Terrace and the Swing Bridge, *c.* 1896. The steam-powered barge *Progress*, on its way out to sea, passes the paddle tug *Rainbow*, which was built on the Thames in the 1860s, and is seen here tied up at the 1892 extension to the Trawl Basin. Much has changed over the intervening hundred or so years since this photograph was taken; the single-storey prefabricated Yacht Club pavilion on the left made way for the present Royal Norfolk & Suffolk Yacht Club headquarters in 1902, while St John's church was to go in the 1970s to be replaced by Levington Court. The two harbourmasters' houses facing each other on either side of the Harbour indicate that the Swing Bridge in use at the time was Lowestoft's first bridge, built in 1830. The northern house, behind the lamp-posts on the side of the Trawl Dock, disappeared with the construction of the Jubilee bridge in 1897; its twin on the south side survived until 1970.

The old Swing Bridge, looking towards the Harbour Hotel and Pier Terrace, photographed by Charles Metcalf, 1896. This was part of the original harbour scheme of the 1830s, but even when the bridge was first opened it was quickly realised that it was too small for the needs of the town. Surprisingly, it lasted over sixty years, surviving Peto's development of the harbour and the New Town Estate.

A cargo vessel being towed into the inner harbour by the tug *Rainbow*, 1897, in a study by a London-based photographer. The two vessels are about to go through the Jubilee Swing Bridge, opened in 1897, Queen Victoria's Diamond Jubilee year, and situated to the seaward side of the old bridge. It was said that this new bridge was the fastest opening in the country.

Henry Seymour Foster, MP for the Northern Division of Suffolk (Lowestoft), late 1890s. The portrait is possibly one of Wilson's first private commissions. H.S. Foster was born at Hornsey in 1855 and educated at the City of London School. He was one of HM Lieutenants of the City of London and Sheriff of London from 1891 to 1892, becoming Member of Parliament for North Suffolk from 1892 to 1910. Knighted in 1918, he died in 1938 aged eighty-three.

Dining room, Foulsham's Hotel, Denmark Road, *c.* 1900. Mainly remembered as the Imperial, Foulsham's faced Lowestoft Central railway station and was one of two large hotels nearby. This family dining room was located on the ground floor. Not only are there menus which extol the virtues of the establishment, but also guides to the varied amusements the town had to offer.

A bedroom, Foulsham's Hotel, *c.* 1900. A typical first-floor bedroom, it was light and airy, and complete with ornate decoration including peacock feather motif carpet. The large windows led out to a south-facing veranda overlooking the railway station.

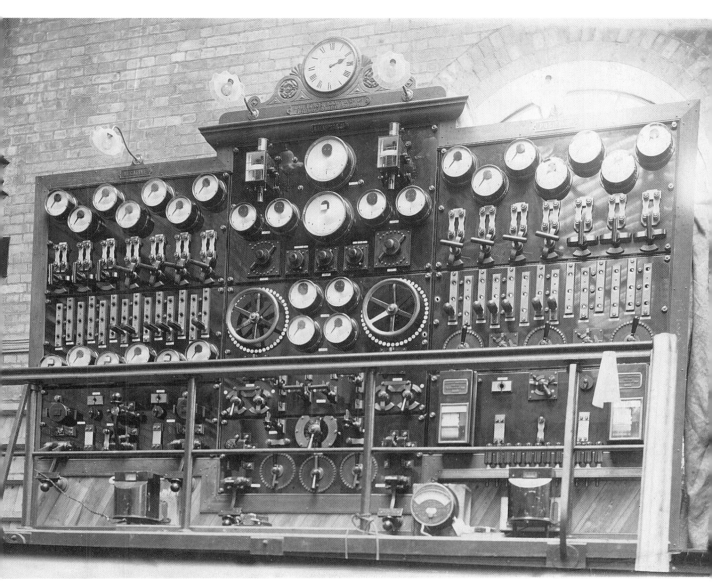

The main switchboard at Lowestoft Electricity Works, Norwich Road, February 1901. Looking like something out of H.G. Wells, this ornate control-board was constructed by Laurence & Scott of Norwich as part of the works on the corner of Rotterdam Road, which was built mainly to supply power to part of the proposed tram system between Caister and Kessingland. The Borough Corporation had given permission to build a small power station as early as 1898, and power was switched on in February 1901. It was used for lighting and heating as well as eventually powering the proposed tramway. In 1901 there were approximately 200 'consumers', as the *Lowestoft Journal* of the day called them; by 1911 this had risen to 1,350. The Norwich Road works were connected to the mains service in 1919, and in 1927 there were some 40 miles of distributing mains in the town. The electric trams started their much-depleted service in 1903, trimmed back mainly because of the railway link between Great Yarmouth and Lowestoft, which opened the same year. The trams only served Lowestoft itself, going as far south as Pakefield and as far north as the town boundary and the newly built Lowestoft North railway station.

London Road Baptist church, *c.* 1899. Considered by many to be one of the best designed churches in the town, it was built on what had once been part of the Grove Estate, cut up into plots and sold for development after the Estate was broken up in 1885. The gates on the left belonged to Grove House, the home of Doctor Henry Walker; the vacant plot on the right became firstly Flood's and, in more recent years, part of Chadd's department store. The church replaced the one located further up London Road, built in 1852 to replace an even earlier building, the old Baptist Meeting House, in the High Street. The original intention had been to enlarge the 1852 building, but following a decision in 1894 to construct a new church, the old one was sold for £1,920. The new building was built by John Ashby and designed by George Baines, an architect responsible for several ecclesiastical buildings in Lowestoft around this period. The foundation stones were laid on 24 February 1898, complete with a sealed container with several local newspapers for that week, a copy of the church magazine, a bill announcing the stone-laying ceremony and a drawing of the old church. Regrettably, this fine church was demolished in the 1970s to make way for the present Boots superstore.

Sparrow's Nest, *c.* 1898. The house is seen as it was almost immediately after being sold to Lowestoft Corporation in 1897. Owned originally by Robert Sparrow of Worlingham, Beccles, it remained much as seen here until the Second World War, when it was hidden from view by the Royal Navy and turned into the Royal Naval Patrol Service headquarters. It was never restored to its former glory and was demolished in 1963, leaving only the wartime buildings and parts of the outer walls intact.

The Model Yacht Pond, Gunton Denes, *c.* 1898. Opened in 1889, it was located between the town allotments (now the Denes Oval) and the North Beach. Boys of all ages would gather there to try out a variety of model boats, from small amateur attempts to quite sophisticated efforts. Official model yacht races were held during the summer months, during which several of the larger models were stored in a hut nearby.

Dutch Suite, Empire Hotel, 1900. Many views can be found of the exterior of this famous hotel; however, these three possibly unique scenes give some idea of its grandiose interior. Designed by Spiers & Pond, the Empire was considered to be the finest seaside hotel in Britain, if not in Europe, and well deserved its description of palatial when it opened in June 1900. Situated on a commanding view on Kirkley Cliff, the hotel accommodated around 300 guests, with the best views to be found on its eastern side facing the sea, where 'full advantage will be had of the pure azone [*sic*] laden, health-giving air that came from the German Ocean', noted an anonymous reporter from the *Lowestoft Journal* after being shown around by the manager, Mr Richardson. It was also noted that much of the carving in the hotel was of solid oak and the furnishings were supplied by Smee & Coby of London. On this somewhat select eastern side there were self-contained family suites consisting of bed and sitting rooms. The hotel also had its own electricity supply, produced by two boilers (also used for cooking and heating), which powered three sets of dynamos. Despite its cost of £150,000, the hotel's life was curtailed by the First World War, after which such luxury could no longer be afforded. The Empire was acquired by the Metropolitan Asylum Board in 1921 as a sanatorium.

The sitting room, *c.* 1900. Situated at the southern end of the hotel in one of the turrets famed for their German helmet-style roofs, this particular room had a glorious view across to Kessingland. Everything was laid on, even down to writing paper on the desk and a piano for those occasional damp and dismal days.

Stories of the grandeur of the hotel lounge were not exaggerated, as this photograph confirms. The small six-sided tables are almost certainly genuine Moorish or Turkish. However, the Empire was built using up-to-date methods, including steel girders as supports, here tactfully integrated into the décor.

Entrance to the Belle Vue Park, north Lowestoft, *c.* 1899. The park was located on the junction between Yarmouth Road and the High Street on what had once been part of the ancient north common. Plans had been made for a public pleasure ground here as early as 1814, but it was only with the development of the Belle Vue estate that the park was finally laid out and opened in 1874. Labelled in the town's handbook for 1906 as 'old Lowestoft's pride' – old Lowestoft being that part of the town north of the bridge – the park stands some 80 ft above sea level, and was complete with pagoda bandstand and thatched park-keeper's lodge, the chimneys of which are seen here peering over the trees. Just inside the entrance, in front of the lodge, were – and still are – the remains of one of Lowestoft's earliest beacons, believed to date back to the sixteenth century. The gates survived until the last war when they and the park's railings were taken away for the war effort. The gate-posts continued to be a prominent feature almost into the 1970s, but were eventually removed, the victim of several accidents: cars unable to take the corner from the High Street into Yarmouth Road occasionally crashed into them. Note the little band of entrepreneurs standing at the top of Cart Score selling ice creams and lemonade.

2

Christopher Wilson

No. 91 London Road North, *c.* 1904. This unique but mutilated postcard shows the Wilson studio (a doctor's residence before 1903) in its earliest days. Leighton's Restaurant is on the other side of the entrance to the Prairie, seen here still with its gate-posts. The little girl is Muriel Wilson.

London Road North, *c.* 1904. The picture was taken by an unidentified photographer near the junctions of Surrey Street and Beach Road, not far from Wilson's old employer's studio at 54 London Road North. Seen here a year after Christopher Wilson opened his own studio (hidden behind the trees centre left), most of these large houses and their grounds were still intact, homes of many of the town's medical profession and proof of Lowestoft's reputation as a successful and thriving health resort. The massive tree near the corner with Surrey Street marked the gardens of Aston Lodge and looked old enough to date back to the early days of the turnpike. Times were changing, however, and in 1904 both sides were quickly becoming commercialised. The trams had arrived, and within a year Jarrold's would open its shop on the corner of Beach Road opposite Aston Lodge. Wilson had left Boughton under a cloud. Not wanting to lose the valuable asset of a good landscape photographer, Boughton had made him an offer, possibly as manager of the Lowestoft studio. But Christopher Wilson had no wish to stay; he wanted to branch out on his own. In 1903 when he was living in the Prairie, he had seen the opportunity literally on his own doorstep, when the house on the corner belonging to Dr George Turner became available. Before long a display case could be found outside enticing all to 'C. Wilson, photographer'.

London Road North after a heavy snow-storm, *c*. 1905. The view was taken in front of the Wilson studio looking north. Those who dared to venture out on this particularly chilly day make their way up the street in between the tram-lines, where there had been attempts to clear the snow. Frank Wheatley's shop on the right marks the southern entrance of the Marina; the same block also shows Boots' first Lowestoft branch at 106 London Road North, taken over when Boughton moved in 1894. Boots would remain here until 1915, when they in turn also moved further down the street. Most of the shops here were destroyed in the Waller raid of January 1942, when in the space of a few seconds a low-flying enemy aircraft dropped a stick of four high explosive bombs, destroying the heart of the town and leaving 70 dead and 114 injured, mostly in Waller's Restaurant. On the left are the gardens of houses also mainly inhabited by the medical profession but interspersed with a handful of shops. Within ten years all of this would change, and those gardens remaining would finally disappear in the early 1920s.

The Wesleyan chapel on the corner of Lorne Park Road and Lawson Road, Kirkley, *c.* 1904. Believed to be designed by G.E. Smith on what was described as a difficult site, the chapel had more than a hint of the hand of architect George Baines and was erected on a site donated by J.J. Colman of mustard fame, next door to Stebbings' dairy. The incumbent at the time was the Rev. Charles Kelly. The chapel included a number of foundation stones, each with the initials of those notables who had laid them. This was one of the older established free church movements in the town. John Wesley himself had frequently visited Lowestoft in the eighteenth century, and the first Wesleyan Methodist chapel was opened by him in 1776 at a cost of £300. As the town expanded so did the free churches, and with the rise of the New Town they eventually established themselves in Kirkley. Many free church members were rising businessmen, reading like a 'who's who' in the town at the beginning of the twentieth century. The Wilsons were no exception, becoming members of the Flensburgh Street Wesleyan chapel when they moved to Ashby Road in the mid-1890s. The Lorne Park Road chapel suffered damage during the Second World War and was eventually demolished.

H. Le Grice, haberdashery, drapery and children's outfitters, 114 and 116 London Road North, *c.* 1905. Lace curtains from 1*s* 11¼*d* to 4*s* 11½*d*; Lowestoft tweed – an acknowledgement of the many Scots visiting the port during the herring season as well as settling here – a bargain at 1*s* 0½*d*, and hats from 1*s* 11½*d*: these were just some of the bargains Le Grice offered, especially to visitors, who were encouraged to 'spend your holiday at Lowestoft', but to 'spend your money at Le Grice's', according to a holiday brochure at the beginning of the new century. From the start many of Christopher Wilson's photographs were used for advertising. A typical example, this scene could be found in the town's official guide for 1906. In the 1920s no. 114 became part of Catling's while no. 116 became an early branch of Marks & Spencer. The building narrowly escaped being destroyed in the Second World War, but was demolished in the 1980s, and is now part of Somerfield's multi-storey car park and supermarket.

Stone-laying ceremony, *c*. 1904. This was at one time believed to be a companion to the scene below; however, the main figures – an elderly man and woman, centre right, both well-dressed – may be members of the Colman family. If so, this appears to be the laying of the foundation stone of one of the many independent or free churches being constructed in the town at the time.

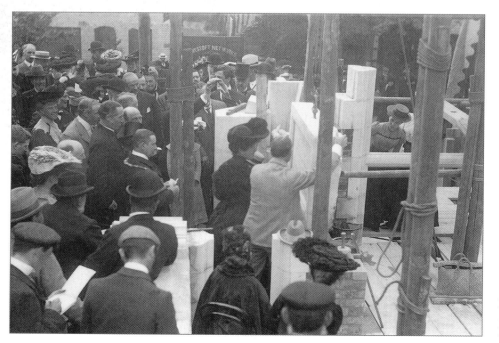

Laying the foundation stone, Carnegie Free Library, Clapham Road, 7 July 1904. The stone was laid by the mayor's wife, Mrs Bourne-Walker. A call had been made nearly twenty years before for a free library in the town, but it was eventually left to the Scottish-American millionaire, Andrew Carnegie, to finance it. Designed by G.W. Leighton and built by G. Howes, the libaray cost £6,000.

Opening of the Sparrow's Nest Gardens Bowling Green, 3 August 1905. The bowling green was purchased by the Borough Corporation out of the Lamplands Fund and opened by the mayor, Ebenezer Tuttle, here standing on the green, and accompanied by his wife and daughters. Its opening was celebrated with an albeit delayed two-day tournament played by clubs mainly from Norfolk and Suffolk. The property also included the house shown in the photograph, built in the 1820s. Many of the town's councillors were prominent local businessmen at this time, and the official party also consisted of R.S. Bradbeer, William Overy and Frederick Spashett. J.W. Brooke was in charge of the town's Parks and Pleasure Grounds Committee, which included the Sparrow's Nest. The weather was very wet, and the mayor had to read his speech under the protection of an umbrella. Although threatened with demolition in the 1960s, when anything old was in danger, the house seen here survived and is now the town's Maritime Museum. The bowling green is also still with us, as popular today as it was when it was first open.

Members of the Lowestoft Arnold Whist Circle, 1906–7. Before the days of radio and when the gramophone was still in its infancy, social gatherings of all descriptions were popular with people of all ages and walks of life. Church groups, theatricals, music making – where occasionally Christopher Wilson would sing and his friend Fred Knights would accompany on the piano – and card games like whist drew large attendances. Popular with local people as well as those coming into the town, they were also seen as opportunities where everyone could get to know each other. This was such a club, believed to have been held at Arnold House in the High Street. The Wilsons, like other couples lately arrived in the town, joined several of these clubs, and who should record such groups but Christopher Wilson, the professional photographer. He was a man who took his time, making sure everyone was in the right place for that second or two exposure on what was a large plate camera. Christopher's wife, Agnes, can be seen seated in the second row, third from the right, holding the nine of clubs, looking somewhat fed up and wishing the thing was over!

A group of young girls dressed in Japanese costume, photographed by Harry Jenkins, January 1908. In the second row, standing next to the woman and first from the right, is the little form of Muriel Wilson, then about nine years old. This particular photographic postcard was addressed to Mrs Capps of Windsor Road – a lady who in her day was an avid collector of postcards.

Coronation Day, 22 June 1911. Photographed from the Royal Hotel, children in their Sunday best and men in their military uniforms mix with the boy scouts, all gathered on the Royal Plain to celebrate the crowning of George V. The celebrations culminated in the lighting of a grand bonfire. Among the crowd are Agnes and the two children, and somewhere in the centre is the mayor, T.E. Thirtle.

LT 437 *Fortuna* passing the South Pier, *c.* 1909. Owned by R.S. Gouldby, this was one of the well-known 'woodbines', so called because the funnels reminded the Edwardians of a famous cigarette brand of the time. One of the earliest recorded attempts of fishing from a steam-powered vessel took place at North Shields in 1877. The first steam-powered vessel built at Lowestoft was the *Consolation* in 1879. Richards' first steam-powered fishing boats appear to have been the *Test* and the *Adventurer*. Despite the cost of the new vessels, the number of new sail-powered fishing boats was in decline by the end of the 1890s, although a handful were still being built for owner-skippers as late as the 1920s. Despite early teething troubles the new vessels soon proved their worth, especially as they were faster and not so prone to the whims of the weather. They could leave port on a calm day while others had to wait for a favourable wind, or for a steam tug to take them out of the harbour. By the 1912 herring season practically all the drifters landing at Lowestoft were steam-powered.

H.H. Chaplin's hardware emporium, 103 London Road North, *c.* 1910. Regimented rows of prams, chairs and mangles are displayed on the site of the old Barrett photographic studio (seen on page 9), which had gone by 1898. These premises were later taken over by J.A. Sturton Ltd, and after the last war a new shop was built for Timpson's Shoes (now Shoe Zone) on its forecourt. Amazingly, the house to the left survives; in the early 1900s it belonged to dentist Ernest Horne, and like other houses in London Road North, its gardens have long been replaced by shops. The line of trees on the right marks the Beeches, later to become part of the London Road North entrance to the bus station in Gordon Road. The tower in the distance is that of the Church of Our Lady Star of the Sea.

The cast of *The Gondoliers*, Lowestoft Amateur Operatic Society, December 1905. This was an early outing of what later became the Lowestoft Amateur Operatic & Dramatic Society, and Wilson, being theatrically inclined himself, quickly learned the advantage of having a studio not far from the Marina Theatre. The performance was produced for Christmas 1905, and the *Journal* reporter of the time thought the performance 'capital throughout'. He complimented the infant company on sticking close to the score with 'no vulgar, nor topical yarns', concluding that if 'this talented company' kept together 'they should do greater things in the future'. Unfortunately he forgot to mention the names of the cast, beyond that of their 'trainer' R.C. Luxton. The performances went on for five consecutive nights. The Friday was a very colourful affair, as the Marina offered a 'half-price night' to any naval or military men who attended wearing their uniforms.

R.J. Crowe as Gaspard, before 1914. Although the production is not recorded, this is a piece of theatrical work that Christopher Wilson must have really relished! There is more than a hint of both photographer and sitter enjoying themselves here. A large framed hand-coloured print of this study once graced the studio, but in later years it was relegated to the youngest child's bedroom!

This portrait of H.R. Allerton as Antonio in Shakespeare's *Merchant of Venice* in 1908 was sent as a Christmas card. The theatre in which Mr Allerton was performing is not recorded, but was most likely the Marina. The portrait may be of an amateur actor, Henry Reeve Allerton, a solicitor and commissioner for oaths at 66 London Road North, now part of Chadd's.

The Clyffe, Corton, *c*. 1908. Built by J.J. Colman in 1869, it was situated 1½ miles north of Lowestoft and stood on top of a cliff, with a sheer drop covered with grass down to the beach below. Enlarged in 1874, it was considered to be the most easterly inhabited building in England. Unused after 1915, it was finally demolished at the end of the First World War.

Fighting a gorse fire, Lowestoft Denes, *c*. 1908. The photograph was taken from Gunton Cliff. The Denes were a popular camping ground, especially with the Territorial Army. Gorse fires in the height of summer were a constant hazard, especially as one spark could do considerable damage. The fire appears to have started some distance away from the camp. Both Territorials and guests are fighting to control the blaze.

Primitive Methodist Conference delegates on the steps of the Elim church, St Peter's Street, 16 October 1911. The three-day conference had been held at the recently enlarged church of St Peter's not far away. The main subject on the agenda centred around children's welfare. A reception the previous Saturday was presided over by Alderman Adam Adams, who welcomed delegates from all over East Anglia to the town. The final day also saw Alderman Adams, who had laid the foundation stone of the Elim church in 1876 and was never the most popular of figures with the people of Lowestoft, spend part of the day's meeting promoting abstinence. This was a bit difficult in a town with two large breweries, and in an area where almost every street had at least one public house in it! The conference ended on Tuesday 17 October.

The charred remains of Richard Leach's hardware store on the corner of Suffolk Road and London Road North, Saturday 25 March 1911. The fire broke out at around midnight the evening before and quickly spread through the building, fed by the stock of paints, oil, varnish, kerosene and wallpaper. High winds assisted in the destruction, which was first noticed by PC Perriman when he was talking to Fred Gilbert of the Hippodrome, Battery Green Road. The shop was a heap of smouldering ruins within an hour of the alarm being raised. Stead & Simpson, next door in London Road North, and Tuttle's store opposite in Suffolk Road, were in imminent danger of catching fire. Seeing that it was impossible to save Leach's premises, the local fire brigade concentrated on containing the blaze: this took three hours. In the end it was estimated that around £5,000-worth of damage had been done. Praising Captain T.E. Thirtle and his men, the *Journal* made the observation that ten years before the same fate had befallen Leach's High Street branch, leaving readers to draw their own conclusions.

1

Lowestoft
1914 to 1933

Durrant's Electrical Engineers, 4 Suffolk Road, early 1920s. The advent of radio and the rise of electricity as a cheap successor to gas are clearly on show here. Mr Durrant's shop hours are of note – closing any time between 6 and 9 pm. Mr Tench had his musical instrument and gramophone record shop here before the First World War.

South Pier Pavilion, 1915. Lowestoft was subjected to occasional Zeppelin attacks during the First World War, and in such a raid in April 1915 the Pavilion fell victim to shelling. At the time it housed naval personnel. Although the exterior looked only slightly scarred, the interior suffered considerable chaos.

German submarine U28 in the Yacht Basin, December 1918. The vessel only visited the port for two days. Note the British ensign flying above the German naval flag – and the two boys.

The South Pier Pavilion, the morning after the Zeppelin attack of April 1915. Apart from smashed windows, little gives any indication of the damage inside. Two official cars stand nearby; by now the war had become mechanised, and the horse had been forsaken for the internal combustion engine.

Victor Wilson in the uniform of the Royal Flying Corps, *c.* 1917. Born in September 1896, he was one of the first pupils at Lowestoft Secondary Modern School as well as a member of the town's first scout group. With a talent for working in wood, he also assisted his father as photographer. Like many young men who went off to fight and survived the ordeal, he did not come out of the war unscathed.

Muriel Wilson, 1918. Then aged eighteen, she was born in 1899, approximately a year after the family moved into the Prairie. There was a wide age difference between Muriel and her younger sister Joan. Muriel, like her brother, took after her mother's side of the family whose ancestors were believed to be Huguenot refugees. The first to marry, she eventually settled in Canterbury.

Joan Agnes Wilson, 1918. Born on 28 August 1917 at a private nursing home in Pakefield Street, she was baptised at St Peter's, Kirkley. As well as seeing an addition to the family, 1917 was also a year that saw the Wilson family fortunes flourish. The youngest of Christopher and Agnes' three children, Joan would become her father's favourite model for the next twelve years or so.

Steam coasters *Melcombe Regis*, *Salcombe Regis* and *Marjorie Mellonie*, Chambers' yard, 1921. Despite an immediate postwar slump, one or two shipyards quickly managed to adapt, as seen here at the John Chambers yard in Harbour Road. Built for a Welsh owner, the *Salcombe Regis* ended up trading along the Argentine coast and travelling up the Rio Plata.

An ex-military lorry with P.W. Watson bodywork, *c.* 1920. The end of the First World War meant that large numbers of unwanted military lorries came on to the market. Many coach-building concerns, like Watson's, saw an opportunity to diversify, either turning them into buses (as did United bodyworks at Laundry Lane), or adapting them for other uses. Thought to be a Dennis, this lorry was part of an early local van-hire service.

Chambers' steel building shipyard, Lake Lothing, early 1920. On the slipway is the SS *Wynstone*, the first all-steel vessel to be launched after the Armistice. Built for Stone & Rolfe, Swansea, and launched in May 1920, the *Wynstone* had the distinction of being the largest steel vessel built in Lowestoft at the time. A simple screw, self-trimming type, she was capable of carrying 760 tons dead weight. Also on the slipway are SS *Emlynton*, launched in June 1920, and SS *Portlaurie*, launched in July 1920, both built for Emlyn, Jones & Company, Cardiff. Like other shipbuilders in the port, Chambers also built many fishing boats, and, like its rival Richards', quickly adapted to the arrival of steam. Chambers' Chronicle for 1920 states that 72 sailing drifters were constructed up to 1919 as against 278 steam drifters. The First World War was the yard's busiest period, with 750 vessels either fitted out or repaired. As well as commissions for the Admiralty, Christopher Wilson spent the war years mainly at Chambers' yard while Agnes ran the studio. Although original photographs from this period appear not to have survived, Wilson may have taken several photographs featuring their war work and used in Chambers' own house journal in the 1920s. He continued photographing for the shipyard, thus being able to stave off some of the recession which affected the town immediately after the war.

Plater's shop, Number 3 yard, John Chambers' boatyard, Lake Lothing, *c.* 1921. Workmen look on as a steel angle is shaped by hand. A superb study by Wilson, this is considered to be one of his finest. The Number 3 yard specialised in building steel ships, notably cargo vessels, and was capable of handling vessels up to 250 ft long. By the early 1920s Chambers' had three yards – this, the engineering division, was located in Harbour Road. Number 1 yard was near Laundry Lane and Number 2 yard was situated at Horn Hill. Not all vessels were built of steel, and Chambers' still maintained an extensive wood covering 300 acres near Worlingham, Beccles. In its heyday the yard had a total of 20 acres at Lowestoft with a frontage of approximately 2,000 ft. The yard closed in 1930.

S.T. Stangroom, stationer and bookseller, 1922. Long before he became known as an estate agent, S.T. Stangroom began his career as a stationer, taking over the old-established business of C.H. Hayes, 92 London Road North, in late 1922. In this study of the shop, Letts' diaries for 1923 were the order of the day, along with Christmas annuals such as *Chatterbox* and *Children's Delight*. Lots of pamphlets are on view, giving advice on preparations for the festive season, and then as now many of the magazines were aimed at women readers. By 1930 Stangroom had moved to 121 London Road North, and was also an auctioneer. As an estate agent he would remain at that address until the 1970s. Bonsall's the jewellers occupied 92 London Road North by 1936. Next to Waller's Restaurant, it was among those destroyed in the Waller raid of January 1942, when both Mr and Mrs Bonsall lost their lives.

LT 608 *Nine Sisters*, a Richards steam drifter built in 1910 for R.Read. By the 1920s, when this photograph was taken, she was in the hands of T.B. Belton of Oulton Broad.

LT 1222 *Thyme* about to pass the pier-heads into the harbour, late 1920s. One of the last sailing smacks built by Richards', she was constructed in 1921 for the Thyme syndicate. Weighing 31 tons, she was also powered by motor.

Henry Pike's tobacconists, 139 London Road North, 1920s. Two families, Norton and Pike, were prominent in Lowestoft as tobacconists in the early years of the last century. Situated next to the Lowestoft Water & Gas Company, Henry Pike's emporium was not far away from the Victoria Arcade, built on the site of the old Baptist church. In an era when smoking was considered the height of masculine fashion – although, admittedly, ladies did smoke in private – this display appears to concentrate on the endless variety of pipes then available, as well as a myriad of brands of cigars, tobacco, matches and cigarettes; the latter containing those much sought-after 'ciggy cards', once so fiercely fought for in many a school playground. Situated between Regent Road and Milton Road East, and built in about 1900, Pike's shop was among the many on this site, now part of Westgate's, to be destroyed during the Second World War. Only Walker's Stores, the *Eastern Daily Press* and *Lowestoft Journal* offices and part of Morling's were left standing on this part of London Road North.

Durrant & Powell, funeral directors, 162 London Road North, early 1920s. Opposite E.J. Morling's music store, this shopfront dated back to the late 1890s. It was next to H.G. Rogers, stationers and publisher of the well-known series of Lowestoft postcards by Harry Camburn. This area was part of the expansion of the town southwards from the High Street. Like the photographic studios, funeral directors and undertakers saw an increase in trade during the First World War, and not just in the war years. This and other similar establishments were the final resting places of many who suffered the psychological scars of battles such as the Somme, their wounds, or gas poisoning, finally succumbing to their fate years afterwards. The actual date of this photograph is uncertain. By the late 1920s it is possible that one of the partners, Powell, had moved to 81 Beccles Road, later to become 221 St Peter's Street. Kay's the grocers by the 1930s, these premises and much of the surrounding block were destroyed by bombing in 1941.

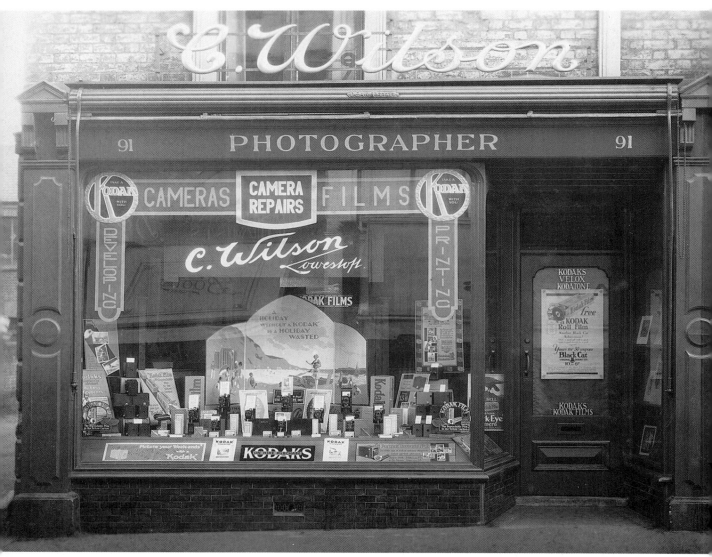

The Wilson studio window in London Road North crammed full of Kodaks and Kodak products, early 1920s – before the front of the shop was altered later in the decade. After the First World War the rapid rise of snapshot photography seriously affected most professional studios, and not only in Lowestoft. Many people saw no reason why they should pay up to 2 guineas for a set of photographs when they could easily obtain them themselves with a box camera costing around 5s, an eight-exposure film for another shilling, and a further 9d to have it developed and printed. Kodak was the largest supplier of cheap box cameras on the market, and just like other studios in the town, the Wilsons became agents for developing and printing amateur snapshots. At Victor's suggestion the old coach house in the Prairie was converted to take the relevant equipment. On the shop door is a poster promoting Black Cat cigarettes (6d for ten), enticing all to save coupons for a Kodak film.

The Wilsons at home, 91 London Road North, mid-1920s. This was an experimental photograph using artificial light, taken in their living room on the first floor. Victor sits on the left, while Christopher Wilson leans with his elbow against the mantelpiece, cigarette in hand, and Agnes sits with that 'seen it all before' look! The table in front of the group, on which Christopher's tobacco jar rests, was also used for wet-mounting photographs. The pictures on the wall are of Victor as a young boy. The round mirror has long since disappeared, but the clock and the jar on the bookcase are still in the family. I suspect, from the way that he is sitting, that Victor took the photograph. Of the other two children, Muriel had married by now, and Joan, still a young child, was most likely in bed.

The cast of *Veronique* on the stage of the Marina Theatre, January 1923. This was a highly acclaimed production by the Lowestoft Amateur Operatic and Dramatic Society of what was a popular light opera. The cast included W.E. Durrant, Violet Foster, Eileen Preston and Gladys Scarff.

The cast of *Tom Jones*, April 1926. The same society went one better at the Marina Theatre three years later, with their rendition of Edward German's musical adaptation of Henry Fielding's book, held in aid of Lowestoft Hospital and the Lowestoft Fishermen's Widows & Orphans Fund. Even the costumes were considered the last word in perfection. Ivan Kittle, who played Tom Jones, came in for praise, as did Vera Meek as Sophia. The furnishings were supplied by Smith's and Camp's.

Edward Benjamin Britten, September 1923. Seated in his South Lodge school uniform, young Benjamin was not as keen as brother Robert or his sister Beth to have his portrait taken, preferring either to play his piano or kick a football around in the street. However, one portrait succeeded – to become in future years Christopher Wilson's most famous image.

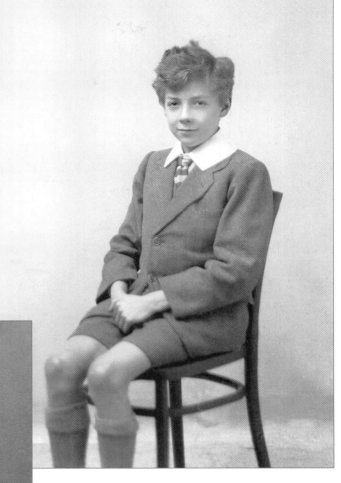

Robert Victor Britten, c. 1923. Born in 1877, he was trained as a dental surgeon at Charing Cross Hospital and came to Lowestoft in 1905. He set up his practice firstly in Marine Parade, and then, in 1909, at Kirkley Cliff Road. There were four children, of whom Benjamin was the youngest. R.V. Britten died in 1934, just as his son was starting to make his mark on the musical world.

The museum room, Carnegie Public Library, Clapham Road, 1920s. For many years this was the nearest the town had to a proper museum. The library had given over space to a collection of memorabilia dating back as far as the Dutch Wars of the seventeenth century. There was also a small collection of Lowestoft china retrieved from the old factory site in 1902, but for the ordinary man and woman the most important exhibits were those of the recent war. Here, the library had put together a collection which consisted of naval battle souvenirs and memorabilia from the Zeppelin and sea attacks on the town. This corner of the room included shrapnel and a damaged weather vane, all bearing witness to either the Zeppelin raids of 1915 and 1916, or the German sea bombardment of the town in April 1916, the latter also graphically shown by the framed photographs on the wall. A prominent position is given to the portrait of Tom Crisp VC. His story, of how he stayed with his boat after being attacked by a German submarine, saving his crew, which included his young son, and going down with his ship, has become seafaring legend. The portrait seen here fortunately survived the war and is now in the Lowestoft Maritime Museum at the Sparrow's Nest.

Carnegie Public Library, Clapham Road, 1920s. This corner of the same room shows souvenirs and photographs, again mainly with a naval connotation. Lifebelts from the *Hirose* from Cardiff, HMS *Speedy* and the German battleship SMS *Zeeland* were among a display which included models, weapons and shell cases. At the start of the Second World War some of the Library's collection was put into storage; however, some, including many of the china factory moulds and possibly some of the items shown here, were destroyed when the library and the technical school next door were bombed in March 1941. The public library reopened in the North Flint House in the High Street, originally given to the town as a museum, and then moved to Suffolk Road in 1951. It finally returned to its old site in the mid-1970s. Regretably many of the exhibits that had been stored at Normanston House, once the home of the Leathe family, were either destroyed in the course of time or lost through pilferage when the building was periodically broken into.

Albert Spurgeon, *c.* 1927, when he was awarded the RNLI's silver medal after saving the crew of the smack *Lily of Devon*. Spurgeon had become coxswain to the Lowestoft lifeboat *Agnes Cross* in 1924 and in the following April was called to follow the runaway airship R33 across the North Sea. He continued as coxswain of the *Michael Stephens* in 1939, and saw service at Dunkirk. He was awarded the DSM for his services in the war and retired in 1947.

Coxswain John Sterry Swan OBE being presented with a framed portrait of himself at the helm of the *Agnes Cross*, early 1923. The presentation was made by Gervais Rentoul MP, who is standing on the right of the portrait, at the Loyal Lacon Lodge of Oddfellows at St Margaret's Institute, Alexandra Road. In the centre, behind the portrait, is mayor Alfred Jenner. Swan retired in March 1924 after taking part in the rescue of a total of 258 people. He died in 1937 aged seventy-eight.

St Peter's Scout Troop outside St Peter's church, Kirkley, 1920s. Second row from the front, third from the right, is believed to be George Plant; another member of the Plant family is seated somewhere among the group. Note the boy with the eye-patch (front row, fifth from right).

Arnold's Department Store, 100 London Road North, *c.* 1925. The shop was on the corner of London Road North and the Marina. For a while the town boasted two branches of this Yarmouth store, firstly 95 and 97 London Road North, later to become the site of BHS, and this magnificent structure opposite, originally called Rink House. Built at the end of the nineteenth century for F.R. Wheatley, like many stores in Lowestoft at the time it had its own café, which was entered at the side from the Marina, to the right of the Ford Model T. Behind the car is the Marina Theatre itself. Also seen here is a somewhat truncated Boots displaying two blurred flags. Those who recall the main street before the war will realise that something is missing from Boots and its neighbour, W.B. Cooper – their upper storeys have been doctored out of the photograph back at the studio! Note the tramlines, and the stop conveniently outside the store. After the trams were withdrawn in 1931 a bus stop was placed only a few yards away outside Boots, remaining there until the town centre was pedestrianised in the early 1980s. Apart from the Marina Theatre and the yard on the extreme left, all of these buildings were lost in the Waller raid of January 1942.

The manager and staff of Arnold's branch at 95 and 97 London Road North in carnival mood, 1924 or 1925. Dressed for the annual summer carnival, Mr Borrett sits in the middle, with his wife on the right at the end of the same row. His daughter, Mary, is the little girl seated on the grass.

Father Christmas arriving at Arnold's, December 1925. The motor car had superseded Santa's reindeer on this occasion, when he arrived for his one week 'at home' held every afternoon at Arnold's restaurant. Behind the expectant hordes of children is Arnold's other branch at Lowestoft.

Nos 91 and 93 London Road North, after the renovations of the 1920s. The old gardens on this side of the street had been removed and had by now become part of what was officially called the Broadway – a name which did not last long. The sign in the studio window was made by Victor Wilson. Both premises were by now owned by the Wilsons, who appeared to be not too keen on Langley's having no. 93 next door; mainly, it was said, because the premises were not looked after very well – and, indeed, the upper two floors in this photograph do look as though they were not in use. By 1926, however, St Edmundsbury Co-operative had taken over the shop. What is now long forgotten is that there once was an alleyway between 93 London Road North and Arnold's drapery next door – yet another of the old houses converted to shops. It was to disappear when the Universal Stores were built in the mid-1930s.

W.H. Learner's, 52 London Road North, late 1920s. Gowns, frocks, hats and furs are on show – the height of late '20s fashion, markedly different from those prewar styles in Le Grice's window on page 29. Next door to Boughton's studio, Learner's were to survive until the late 1950s. The premises are now part of the Norwich and Peterborough Building Society.

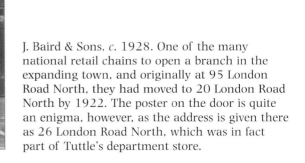

J. Baird & Sons, *c.* 1928. One of the many national retail chains to open a branch in the expanding town, and originally at 95 London Road North, they had moved to 20 London Road North by 1922. The poster on the door is quite an enigma, however, as the address is given there as 26 London Road North, which was in fact part of Tuttle's department store.

P.W. Watson's garage, St Peter's Street, late 1920s. Opposite Clapham Road, it is now the site of Plaisir Place. Watson's had a garage here as early as 1907; however, as coachbuilders, they could trace their history back to the 1840s. They were agents for Wolseley cars, but the car in the centre is, in fact, a brand new bullnose Morris Cowley – a snip at £255.

A motor hearse with coachwork by P.W. Watson, before 1928. The picture was taken on Gunton Cliff – for many years a popular promenade and, for some reason, an ideal spot for coachbuilders to take their latest work to be photographed! The side and tail lights of this vehicle seem to be oil lamps instead of electric; it is very likely that this was a pre-war chassis fitted with a new body.

John Devereux & Sons, 127–30 High Street, 1920s.
Designed by W. Oldham Chambers in the 1860s, this
building was next to the town's market-place, the space on
the left which had originally been a site earmarked for a
town hall that was never built. By the 1920s Devereux's
had become the largest locally owned business in the area,
and eventually survived until the early 1970s.

Devereux's warehouse, *c.* 1924. This was built on the
corner of Old Market Plain and Old Market Street, on the
site of what had once been a row of houses dating back to
the seventeenth century. Devereux's also included what
had been a small chapel located between the warehouse
and the main shop. The van is a Ford Model T, a make
popular with local traders.

Hillcote, Gunton Cliff, 1920s. This was the home of Spencer Love, before the First World War a successful tailor and hosier. It was in the midst of houses belonging to many of Lowestoft's equally successful business fraternity. The conservatory next door belonged to Briar Clyffe, the home since 1904 of Howard Hollingsworth, of Bourne & Hollingsworth fame.

An old fireplace, 1920s.
This photograph is possibly the only record of this late eighteenth-century fireplace. The grate is believed to have been made by a local blacksmith, possibly at the smithy in Old Market Plain. The actual location of the cottage is not known; however, the name Mobbs on the negative suggests it may have been taken either for a local builder, or possibly for A.G. Mobbs at Oulton.

Thomas Henry Thirtle, Honorary Chief Fire Officer, Lowestoft Corporation Fire Service, *c.* 1930. Secretary and Deputy Chief Fire Officer in 1914, Thomas Henry eventually succeeded his father, T.E. Thirtle, becoming Honorary Chief Fire Officer by 1922, a time when Lowestoft had three fire stations. He died in July 1938 aged fifty-six.

All set for an outing, Royal Plain, *c.* 1927. In front of the Royal Norfolk & Suffolk Yacht Club a coachman looks on enviously at the Ford TT bus nearby, one of two about to journey into the nearby countryside of Suffolk and Norfolk on what is believed to be an outing of members from the Lodge of Unity, one of Lowestoft's many masonic lodges. Christopher Wilson had become a member of this lodge in 1917, and on this occasion was also on board recording their venture into the country. The bus on the left appears to be one built locally, most likely at P.W. Watson's works in Thurston Road. Behind it is an open charabanc – with everyone wearing hats. How *did* they keep them on when the bus was moving? Because of the numbers of vehicles discarded by the military after the First World War, the 1920s became the era when the internal combustion engine eventually took over from the horse – only two horse-drawn vehicles can be seen here on the Royal Plain. Once the roads echoed to the jingling sounds of harness bells as horses took wagons packed with happy holidaymakers around nearby villages. After the war those same country lanes reverberated to the sound of the petrol engine.

South Pier bandstand, *c.* 1930. For many years in front of the Pavilion, the old bandstand was eventually moved a few feet on to the pier itself. Now more weatherproof, it also protected the bandsmen from the occasional inclement weather, and included loudspeakers which ensured that the band of the day could be heard over a wider distance – albeit here on a cold day when hardly anyone was on the pier!

Prince of Wales Challenge Cup, Royal Norfolk & Suffolk Yacht Club, August 1928. A race for 14ft dinghies first run at Cowes in 1927, for its second year it was held off the coast at Lowestoft. Thirty-nine dinghies competed and the race was won by Uffa Fox in *Avenger*, a vessel built to his own design. By the late 1930s the cup was to be won at least eight times by the Yacht Club.

Lowestoft Central railway station and Station Square, *c* 1929. The railway station had been the centre of the town since 1847 for those coming to Lowestoft to work or to live, for a holiday or for health reasons. As they stepped out of the station in the late 1920s, they were greeted with the choice of the Imperial Hotel, known earlier in the century as Foulsham's Hotel, opposite in Denmark Road, or the imposing Suffolk Hotel, partly seen on the right and built on the site of the earlier coaching inn of the same name. Between the Imperial and the Suffolk was Bevan Street, and in the foreground were the railway lines from the station goods yard crossing London Road North with its overhead tram wires, into the Fish Market. Within two years the trams would be gone, superseded by motor coaches and buses, two of which are seen here, albeit facing the wrong way for today's traffic. The 1B to Southwold stands in front of the railway station while another bus waits at the Denmark Road side of the new traffic island, ready to go to Oulton Broad. Both were run by United, a local company later to become Eastern Counties.

Imperial Hotel, Denmark Road, *c.* 1929. For the best part of sixty years this had been the first building that greeted the newly arrived as they came out of the station. Not long before this photograph was taken the view would have been obstructed by Crossley House, then on the corner of Denmark Road and London Road North, and demolished in 1928. The site was then used as a traffic island, mainly as a halt in London Road North for trams, and on the other two sides firstly for United and later for Eastern Counties buses. Looking across from London Road North towards Denmark Road, almost every house from the Imperial to Junction Passage was a boarding house. Behind the solitary telegraph pole is one of Lowestoft's well-remembered trams on the line leading from the tram depot in Rotterdam Road. In 1941 a bomb blew a large crater in front of the Imperial, killing several servicemen; later that year part of the hotel and several of the houses behind the tram were destroyed by a direct hit.

Marine Parade, *c. 1930*. Built by Sir Morton Peto as 'second-class' residences as part of his New Town Estate, historically the terrace had held court to a number of famous men. Dickens was reputed to have stayed there, the photographer Peter Henry Emerson was known to have lodged there, and George Davison, the eminent Secessionist photographer and philanthropist, joint founder of the 'Linked Ring' and later to become managing director of the English branch of Kodak, was born there. Under the fifth chimney from the right is no. 9, the boarding house bought by Christopher and Agnes Wilson in 1927, partly as a result of the instability of the studio business at the time and partly because of illness in 1924, when Christopher contracted pneumonia and the studio nearly closed. The boarding house also helped Victor, who, although talented and assisting his father, was not a successful businessman. As they were no strangers to putting up boarders, firstly at the Prairie, then above the studio, their acquisition of a boarding house kept the Wilson family financially secure. Boarding houses were the town's third largest industry; in fact it was considered the most stable in the town. The photograph is taken in front of the Royal Hotel; opposite Marine Parade are the trees of the houses on the Esplanade. Today, however, Marine Parade directly faces the sea.

The roof of the Playhouse Theatre from the back garden of 9 Marine Parade, August 1932. Originally an auctioneer's, this single-storey building peering over the top of the Wilson garden shed became the New Theatre in 1927. Renamed the Playhouse, sound films arrived in 1930 – this particular week saw James Cagney and Joan Blondell starring in *Larceny Lane*.

Unloading cargo from the SS *Frieda Rehder, c.* 1930. For the time being, at least, Lowestoft remained a busy port, exporting herring to the Baltic countries, although not in such great quantities as she once had, and in return bringing in a variety of European goods ranging from food to machine parts. The Depression, however, was not far away.

LT 76 *Excel* moored at the North Quay, *c.* 1930, on the same day as the above. She was a drifter-trawler owned by Kittiwake Ltd, one of the many subsidiaries of Frederick Spashett at Waveney Chambers. Weighing 43 tons, she was built in 1907.

An incident at the Fish Market entrance, *c.* 1931. The early 1930s were a difficult time for Lowestoft. Unemployment was rife and even affected the fishing industry. The reason for this incident is not recorded, but it appears that the market had been cordoned off. Men are attempting to remove the barricade to allow a lorry to get through.

Another photograph of the same incident: the lorry is now through, and two men are standing on its back addressing the crowd. It is possibly a union meeting, but there is no sign of a police presence. Four years later, in 1935, things had still not improved. There were still over 1,500 men out of work.

Doris, a houseboat built in 1931 by J.W. Brooke for Mr Edward Evans, who later became MP for Lowestoft. Seen here on Oulton Broad not long after its launch, it was 65 ft in length and luxuriously fitted out. Based in London for many years until severely damaged by fire and left to sink at its moorings, it was rescued in the 1980s and restored at Oulton Broad.

Doris sitting on the slipway at Brooke's yard in Harbour Road, 1931. This is a rare record of the houseboat immediately prior to its launch. A flat-bottomed craft, she was designed for inland waters such as the Broads and parts of the Thames.

The interior of *Doris*, 1931. Very spaciously laid out and fitted with electric light, as this view of the bow saloon shows, the boat emphasised the high standard of workmanship for which Brooke's were internationally renowned.

The stern saloon of *Doris*, 1931. The high quality of fixtures and fittings continued throughout the vessel. With bright flowers, loom chairs and cushioned settee, one would almost expect to find Noel Coward sitting in the corner. Steering and controls were at the stern, which can be seen through the doorway.

A trailer chassis by J. Harrison's, Battery Green Road, *c.* 1931. Harrison's was one of several engineering works in the town concentrating not only on shipping but also on the emerging motor industry. By now petrol was no longer available solely in cans, but also by pump at the roadside, as here. Pratt's Commercial was the fuel in this case. Shell oil cost between 1*s* 8*d* and 1*s* 11*d*.

A Brooke engine, possibly at Adrian Works, Alexandra Road, 1931. This is an undoctored photograph possibly of a prototype of one of the Brooke series of engines that was announced the following year. It also shows part of the workshop.

Brooke 44 customs launch alongside the yard at Harbour Road, 1929. Brooke's skill was in fast reliable motorboats, and in 1929 the Brazilian government placed an order for thirty customs launches and three customs cutters for Rio de Janeiro. It was the largest foreign order for the yard up to that time.

Brooke Dominion engine, 1931. A 5 hp two-cylinder petrol engine, it was one of a series of new marine engines announced for 1932. Top of the range was the 10 hp four-cylinder Empire. A new six-cylinder diesel model was also announced for that year.

Alderman George Shadforth resplendent in his mayoral robes, 1929. Holding office for two terms, 1929–30 and 1930–1, he was also a member of the Baptist church. He lived at Boston Lodge, dying there in July 1935 aged seventy-four.

Below: Ernest William Tooke, with his mother (centre) and wife. A pastry cook, Ernest Tooke had his bakery at 17 Bevan Street, now part of Bevan Street West. His shop was next to James Garrod's, the last saddle and harness makers in Lowestoft.

Sir Gervais Rentoul KC. A lawyer by profession, he became MP for Lowestoft in 1922 and quickly made his name in politics. A respected figure in the town, in his time Lowestoft regained much of its pre-First World War eminence as a resort and port of repute. Knighted in 1929, he eventually lost his seat in the 1931 General Election. He died in 1946 at the age of eighty-one.

St Margaret's church silver photographed for a handbook written by the Rev. H.J. Enraght and published in 1932. At one time Lowestoft greatly revered its early seafaring and merchant past, which had historically contributed much to the town. Many of its merchant families, including the Mighells, Arnolds and Wildes, donated items to the parish church, and they are among the plate shown here, some dating back to the 1670s.

Arnold's Drapery Store, 100 London Road North, *c.* 1930. A small crowd, either staff or eager customers, gathers on a dull morning, waiting for the doors to open. A first prize winner of that year's Lowestoft Carnival Shopping Week, the shop had put everything into its window display, part of which appears to show costumes which may have used in one of the plays or shows at the Marina Theatre not far away. Arnold's café had become a popular meeting place with many of the town's younger adults who would soon include Joan Wilson, now in her teens. Based in Great Yarmouth, Arnold's two Lowestoft branches were amalgamated in 1932; however, even this branch would soon close, becoming Fifty Shilling Tailors by 1938. Chipperfield's then moved on to the upper floors after selling their shop opposite to the Odeon cinema chain in 1935. Tramlines are still prominent in this view, as are the overhead wires. Also seen here on the right is Boots Cash Chemists next door – this time at its full height. Sold to Boots in late 1914, and opened up in 1915, the shop's upper two bays were removed to take the unusual arcade front all Boots stores had at the time.

Joan Wilson's fifteenth birthday party, Esplanade, Kirkley, 1932. Christopher, assisted by daughter Muriel, organised a party for Joan's birthday in August that year on the sands of the South Beach in front of the family hut on the Jubilee Esplanade. Friends and relatives were invited and Christopher, naturally, recorded the day. Back row, left to right: Mrs Trimmer, Wendy Trimmer, Joan Wilson, Mary Fairhead, Terry Hutson. Middle row: Minnie Gribble, Muriel Anderson (Joan's sister), Nancy Lewis with Michael Anderson on her lap, and Roy Pankhurst. Front row: Eric Hutson with Dandy, John Anderson, Hubert Gribble and Olga Maul. The Hutsons ran a butcher's and dairy in Pakefield; John and Michael Anderson were Muriel's children. Nancy Lewis came from the family of drapers and costumiers in London Road North; and Mary Fairhead's father ran the Gourock Rope Company in Battery Green Road. Hubert Gribble would eventually die at the hands of the Japanese. At the time of writing John Anderson is a retired doctor living in New Zealand. The party had an underlying tinge of sadness as one person was missing – Agnes.

Agnes Brumby Wilson, *c.* 1930. Agnes was born at Tetney, Lincolnshire, in 1875, her middle name stemming from a village near Scunthorpe. She had fallen ill in 1932, and although she was sent to a local nursing home to recuperate, her health continued to decline. She died of heart disease four days before her fifty-eighth birthday in January 1933. It was effectively the end of the studio at 91 London Road North.

Below: Lowestoft Co-operative Society annual staff dinner, 19 January 1933, at the Grand Hotel nine days after Agnes' death. The Co-operative movement had been in the town since 1890, although the Co-op factory itself was only four years old, having taken over Maconochie's in Waveney Drive in 1929. Victor Wilson is believed to have taken the photograph.

4

Lowestoft 1934 to 1946

A tranquil early morning sunrise in the warm summer months of the 1930s. This idyllic view of the sea at low tide, with the sun just breaking over the South Pier and its Pavilion, emphasises why the town rightfully earned its motto 'Where the sun meets the sea'.

London Road North, early 1937. After the death of Agnes, Christopher Wilson moved his studio down to the family boarding house in Marine Parade, and by early 1935 had leased out the old shop to H.G. Hannant; it became the first Hannant toy and wool shop north of the Swing Bridge. Thomas Gore had already moved down from the High Street into the premises next door, and the old building was by now starting to look slightly lost beside more recent developments nearby, especially the adjacent Odeon, opened in great splendour in January that year on the site of N.E. Chipperfield's ironmongers, and the Universal Stores built earlier in the decade on the site of the old Arnold's store opposite the Marina. Once Leighton's restaurant before the First World War, the Odeon itself was built by D. Leighton & Sons, a local building contractor with a branch in Potter's Bar, and who were responsible for many of the Odeon cinemas in the country during the 1930s. The car is a Ford.

The Playhouse Cinema from the rear garden of 9 Marine Parade, after 1933. The sun is out and the flowers are in bloom in this comparison view of the rebuilt Playhouse, opened in April 1933 and now in the height of art deco fashion. It was also offering repertory as well as films. In such surroundings as this there was an advantage to having the studio and the boarding house together under one roof.

Early morning fish auctions, looking in the direction of the Herring Sale Ring, Lowestoft Fish Market, mid-1930s. A large part of the market seen here survived the Second World War and remained virtually unchanged (including some of the barrows seen here) up to the late 1970s. Arthur Easto's, near the camera, survived beyond the Second World War, although his stand did not – suffering damage in 1941.

Looking in the opposite direction to the previous picture: fish was now sold mainly in boxes and in kit (10 stone) barrels instead of loose on the market floor. Much of this section, however, was destroyed during the war. Also here is Larvin & Co.'s stand. In 1947 they were to become part of Explorator, a pioneer in fish delivery by road, a system which eventually ousted rail.

Loading herrings for export, mid-1930s. During the herring season every part of the town was given over to its preparation, packing and loading, including the ground next to the Yacht Club. From September until the season ended in December, it is no exaggeration to state that the whole town became one massive fish-processing plant, mainly for the European market.

Looking from the grounds next to the Yacht Club towards Waveney Road, two men watch barrels of fish being loaded aboard a cargo vessel in the mid-1930s. Ships of all sizes seem to have been used, and here all sense of caution appears to have been forsaken as the barrels are stacked ever higher.

Waveney Dock from the North Extension, *c.* 1935. The building visible over the roofs of the market is Pryce's 'castle', built in 1933. During the 1930s trawlers generally had a bad time, especially those remaining smacks that were run by owner-skippers or were owned by individuals with only one or two boats. Among those moored here are LT 302 *Flower of Devon* and LT 759 *Crimson Rose*, both owned by Miss Painter of Haward Street.

Great Grimsby Coal, Salt & Tanning's carnival float LT 7777, possibly for the Jubilee of 1935. Standing outside their offices and works in Battery Green Road, now the site of the Job Centre. The float was built around a car or small lorry and disguised as a steam drifter. Fishermen being very superstitious, in reality Lowestoft fishing boat numbers only went as high as LT 1299 – any vacant numbers were reused as and when needed.

Bingham's Central Bakery and Tea Rooms, opposite the Triangle Market, July 1935. Like Turner's next door it was all dressed up to celebrate the King's Silver Jubilee and the Golden Jubilee of the Borough of Lowestoft. It consisted of four days of festivities and fun, although the weather did not always join in.

The junction of Old Nelson Street and London Road North, July 1935. The patrolman on point duty is standing in front of Camp's Antiques. The town took mayor Selwyn Humphrey literally when he encouraged everyone to display bunting and flags profusely; as can be seen here, the main street became one long avenue of decorations.

Jubilee celebrations, Thursday 4 July 1935. A procession of trade vehicles started off from Waveney Road at 6 p.m., travelling along Marine Parade, past Christopher Wilson's house and his vantage point on the first floor, towards Pakefield Street and returning along London Road South. Just some of the 110 participants are seen here passing the Royal Hotel and the mayor and his retinue.

The Jubilee celebrations on that Thursday evening in 1935 made for an imposing show. It took one and a half hours to complete the journey – Bridgers excepting! Mann Egerton's entry was their new breakdown lorry complete with a bevy of beautiful young ladies. It took second place in the overall awards for the evening.

Other award-winning displays on that Jubilee Thursday evening in 1935 included W.B. Cooper's float with its spectacular floral crown, followed here by the restrained display of the Master Bakers Association.

General election, St Margaret's Institute, November 1935. P.C. Loftus (left) had taken Sir Gervais Rentoul's seat in Ramsay MacDonald's National Coalition election in 1931. His position was confirmed four years later, when he won a 7,716 majority vote over his rival, Major F.J. Wise (right, about to talk to the crowd), and would remain the town's MP until 1945.

Lowestoft at the height of the summer season, 1930s. Seen from the balcony of the South Pier Pavilion, the centre of the resort – the Royal Hotel – stands proud over all as it had done for some eighty years. The Esplanade is full of holidaymakers and the South Beach is nearly packed.

The paddle-steamer *Marchioness of Breadalbane* leaving the South Pier for a pleasure trip in the mid-1930s. Joining the Belle steamers for a few years before the war, the *Marchioness* took trippers out on short cruises off the coast three times a day during the season. All ceased in September 1939, when the last steamers to dock at Lowestoft brought evacuees from London.

South pier-head light, 1930s. This is a detailed study
of the wooden south light, then nearly ninety years
old. It was one of a pair built by Peto for the original
pierheads of his harbour, and was demolished and
replaced in 1937.

Ready for the off, 1930s. On the South Pier
R.S. Stranack, observing the gathering craft, stands
with percussion gun in hand, preparing to start a
race of Broads One Design yachts, while not far
away for the grand sum of 1s (children 9d) visitors
were tempted to a lively 10 mile trip out to sea on
the pleasure boat *Melba*.

The proclamation of Edward VIII on the Royal Plain, January 1936. King George V died on 20 January, less than nine months after his Silver Jubilee. Proclamation of the new king was announced two days later, and on a cold and wet day crowds gathered on the Royal Plain to hear the mayor, W. Smith, read out the declaration.

Crowds waiting to hear the proclamation of Edward VIII, January 1936. The ceremony only took a few minutes; the proclamation of the new king was read out and was followed by the National Anthem and three cheers for the new monarch. The weather being very cold, the crowd then quickly dispersed.

An incident outside 10 Marine Parade, 1930s, in which a Morris saloon appears to have swerved into another car. The photograph was taken from the entrance of Wilson's house next door. The trees in the gardens opposite are almost bare, indicating autumn. The scene also allows a passing glimpse of both the railings in Marine Parade, mostly removed later, and in particular the unusual diamond-shaped pavements outside the houses of Marine Parade itself.

North Quay, *c.* 1936. The small tripod crane behind the modern larger one, obscured by steam from the piledriver repairing the quay, was demolished in 1938. Its original function was to lift boilers out of the early steam vessels, but in later years it was used for lowering masts. Pier Terrace is framed by the smoke from the nearby barge.

An SS Airline parked near the Royal Hotel, Marine Parade, 1936. Rare enough in its day, it was considered one of the finest looking cars of its time; however, its design was considered too advanced and only 600 were built. Founded in Blackpool in 1921, the initials were believed to have originally stood for Swallow Sidecars. The first cars were built in the late 1920s. In 1945 the company became Jaguar cars.

Harry Jenkins with daughter Margaret, her husband and son at the Thatched Restaurant, Kirkley Cliff, mid-1930s. A fellow photographer based at Pier Terrace, Jenkins came to Lowestoft from Tunbridge Wells in 1896, taking over the long-established studio of H.W. Bevan. His brother Frederick, also a photographer, settled in Southwold in 1900. The oldest studio in Lowestoft, it survived until September 1997. Harry died in April 1952.

A Corporation bus ploughs through floodwater, Tuesday 5 July 1938. This was the result of a summer's downpour the previous evening, when the overflow drains were unable to cope. The bus, built at Eastern Coachworks, is attempting to get to North Parade from Pakefield. Boards are out at an optimistic Playhouse Cinema, mainly advertising the week's big film, *The Great Ziegfeld*, starring William Powell and Myrna Loy.

The flooding in July 1938 extended from the Central garage, seen in the distance, to St John's and even included the rear of the Wilson house in Marine Parade. An Austin 7 van is seen here following in the wake of a car in an attempt to get through the water. Despite recurring flooding, the problem was not rectified until the torrential storm of August 1999.

The Wilson sisters at the family hut on the Jubilee Esplanade, 1937. Muriel stands with her two sons, Michael and John, while Joan sits with her fiancé, Alan Plant, whose father, Henry, was a picture-frame maker and timber merchant. A volunteer fireman at Carlton Road, Alan's career would take off during the war years.

The Martin and Durrant families, *c.* 1937. Pakefield, like Lowestoft, had its own fishing dynasties with their roots going way back into history. Members of two such families are seen here. 'Bo' Martin stands on the left of Joan Wilson, with Archie Durrant in the centre. Both families lived in St George's Road, Pakefield.

The Rev. George Reginald P. Preston MA, *c.* 1937. Educated at Merton College, Oxford, he was rector of St Peter's Church, Kirkley, for twenty-five years, and officiated at the wedding of Joan and Alan Plant in September 1937. Retiring in December 1944 because of ill-health, he died at his home in Gorleston in April 1945 aged seventy-six.

A newly married Alan and Joan Plant on the steps of the Clyffe Hotel, 2 September 1937. The bride's dress was described in the *Lowestoft Mercury* as 'white georgette with long bishop's sleeves and a rouched [*sic*] bodice over a taffeta slip'. Also on the steps of the Clyffe are best man Walter Cook, with Ruth Harrington (left) and Doris Plant (right).

The rear of 91 London Road North from the Prairie, 1938. Early that year H.G. Hannant decided to expand their shop. Demolition at the rear revealed some of the workings of the old studio. The white walls seen on both the ground and first floors, for instance, indicated where the two portrait studios had been. The earlier one had been on the upper floor, and was joined later by a larger studio built in the back yard. The kitchen – indicated by the window on the ground floor facing the Prairie – was occasionally used as a darkroom, while a small room elsewhere housing the domestic gas meter was used to develop negatives! And woe betide anyone using the family loo on the first floor while clients were having their portraits taken – the pipe passed through the ground-floor studio! All was to go in Hannant's expansion.

The Prairie, showing the coach house and rear of 91 London Road North, 1938. Like many of the surviving houses on the west side of the street, it was inevitable that sooner or later it would undergo major changes, none more so than when H.G. Hannant decided to upgrade his shop and to blend with the rest of the neighbouring premises into what had become the town's main shopping centre. The rear of the building was completely demolished, thus enabling Hannant not only to modernise but also to increase shop space. Also seen here is the coach house, a sign of the status of its nineteenth-century owners, which survived the rebuilding. Nos 1 and 2 the Prairie were private houses then, but later John Howard's estate agents. Under the tower of Stella Maris, also known as the Church of Our Lady Star of the Sea, in Gordon Road, is part of the recently built side wall of the Universal Stores, soon to be taken over by Hills & Steele.

London Road North, 1938. A large window now dominated H.G. Hannant's shop, and although considered unsightly in the old studio, it actually fitted in well with the rest of the town centre. In fact, 91 and 93 London Road North were now considered prime sites, being valued at approximately £10,000. Each of the two shops annually brought in £300 alone – and this in an era when the average wage was under £200 a year. The light-coloured plaster-work blended with the adjacent Hills & Steele department store, lately taken over from Universal, and the eighteen-month-old Odeon cinema on the opposite side of the Prairie, once the entrance to a large, almost country, estate, but now looking like the alleyway it had become. Although unhappy with the alterations to his old studio and family home, Wilson's ever-ready artistic eye picked out that one figure, a young woman waiting to cross the road, to lift this into something better than an ordinary record shot.

Hannant's Toy and Wool shop, on the corner of the Prairie, with Gore's the jeweller's next door, 1938. The one-word comment 'After' written in a heavy hand on the back of this photograph says it all. Although unable to return to the scene of his life with Agnes, Wilson was nevertheless unhappy with what Hannant's had done with the old place, in particular the large window in what was once their living room. Toys were now on the first floor, and this tradition continued after Hannant's enforced move after the Waller raid in 1942; however, wools and needlecraft would remain the shop's main business. The shop had now become absorbed into the commercial life of the town centre, but not so the old houses in the Prairie, seen here on the left, with hardly any front gardens and no rear. These houses would survive into the 1980s, when they were finally demolished to make way for the Britten Centre.

The Esplanade and South Beach in the late 1930s, looking across to the Claremont Pier and the South Beach and towards north Lowestoft, Pryce's 'castle' and the gasometer. Hundreds of people are strolling along the Esplanade. In the foreground, and used as a wind guide to the golfers in front of the Thatched Restaurant, is an aerial sock advertising the Kirkley Hotel, from where this photograph was taken. Even more people are on the sands, basking in the late afternoon sun. The Children's Corner and the South Pier continued to be as popular as ever. The majority of Lowestoft's holidaymakers continued to arrive by train but the motor car had started to make its presence felt, as can be seen here near the camera.

By 1937 Lowestoft, like the rest of the country, was feeling the benefits of improved employment, notably in engineering and shipbuilding. Improving times meant that more holidaymakers were able to come to the town. But not all was good news. Fishing, notably trawling, was still suffering, and there was the ominous threat of war in Europe. As early as February 1937 the town was urged to start organising ARPs and to examine the possible need of air-raid precautions. The town's first ARP officer was appointed a year later. War was declared in September 1939.

Christopher Wilson, ARP warden, 1940. Age did not stop those at home from helping in the war effort and it was not long before Christopher was appointed warden for his area in Marine Parade, although he was approaching seventy. Checking to see that the blackouts were being observed, he would occasionally go on patrol with the rector of St John's.

The drifter *Rowan Tree* scuttled at the mouth of the harbour, with HMS blockship *Fidelia* in the background. They were sunk as part of a deterrent to prevent enemy vessels from entering the outer harbour. The sign in front of the north pier-head lighthouse announces that no vessel is allowed out without an official pass.

Clearing debris, Lowestoft Fish Market, April 1941. As Lowestoft had a naval base, as well as considerable shipbuilding and engineering facilities, it was obviously a prime target for enemy aircraft. The town also had the Royal Naval Patrol Service at the Sparrow's Nest, and its population, now somewhat depleted, was replaced mainly by soldiers, sailors and Wrens. The enforced cessation of fishing also gave the local net-making industry a new lease of life producing camouflage nets. The Fish Market itself played host to a diversity of vessels – including MTBs, patrol boats and mine-sweepers. As such, it was obvious that the market and the surrounding area would become a target and it was hit several times. One notable attack occurred in April 1941 when the Waveney Dock, the Trawl Market and shipping off the coast were hit. Christopher Wilson was one of only two official photographers in Lowestoft during the war: Ford Jenkins worked for the Ministry of Information and Wilson for the Admiralty, a position he had also held in the First World War.

Lowestoft Fish Market, April 1941. The Fish Market was attacked at least twice in 1941 with considerable damage being caused. It was while recording these scenes one day that Wilson lost all sense of time, and found himself locked in the Fish Market.

Lowestoft Fish Market, April 1941. There was no fishing out of Lowestoft during the war. The market was closed and the area was commandeered by the Navy for the duration. In this scene at the Waveney Market military and civilian personnel check what was left of one of the prewar wooden offices, now shattered by bombs.

Nos 91 and 93 London Road North after the Waller raid of January 1942, showing the extensive shrapnel and bomb-blast damage which effectively caused a large crack between the first and second floors. Hannant's found new premises further down the road at 56 London Road North, and Gore moved to 63a. Neither returned.

Fire damage, 91 London Road North, after 1942. The shops might have been rebuilt had it not been for a drunken tramp breaking into Hannant's and setting fire to the ground floor. Eventually it became impossible for the War Damages Commission to assess the actual bomb damage caused in January 1942.

Marine Parade, early 1945. On a freezing cold day, with sounds deadened by the snow, a lone soldier braves the elements while two more clear the pavement nearby. Looking from 9 Marine Parade towards the Royal Hotel, at the time HMS *Europa*, and towards the Royal Plain and the Yacht Club, it is apparent that not all the railings had been taken for the war effort; some close by seem to have escaped.

Clearing the South Beach of mines, early summer 1944. With the tide of war turning in Europe and the lifting of the Coastal Ban, civilians and military personnel watch members of the Royal Engineers Mine Disposal Unit check the beach for landmines, prior to relaxation of restrictions that had been in force since 1940. For a few weeks later that summer Lowestoft became as popular as it had been before the war.

Salute the Soldier Week, 27 May 1944. The opening march-past on its way south along London Road North towards the Swing Bridge, from the junction of Beach Road. Pipers are leading a contingent of sailors past Chadd's and Victoria Chambers. The two striped posts at the junctions of Surrey Street and Beach Road were what was left of temporary wartime traffic lights.

Salute the Soldier Week, May 1944. Lord Ironside acknowledges a fellow officer in Marine Parade after arriving to take the salute of the returning march-past after its journey down London Road South and Cliff Road.

Lord Ironside taking the salute near the Esplanade car park, Marine Parade, as a pair of armoured cars returns towards north Lowestoft at the end of the opening day of Salute the Soldier Week. The march-past consisted of military units based at Lowestoft and included units from other services in the town. Also present were Lord Stradbrooke and Lady Somerleyton.

London Road North, May 1944. By now the main street consisted of boarded-up shops and bomb-sites. Looking northwards, Howes' pram works next to Matthes' had closed, but would later become a temporary branch of the Co-op. Several other shops on this side, although shuttered, are open for business. Opposite, not far from Chadd's, are the two surviving shops from the Waller raid, now minus their upper storeys.

VE Day Parade, seen from 9 Marine Parade, 1945. Guides and Brownies march past Naval Headquarters at HMS *Europa*. Ten years before the parade was for the Jubilee, now it was Victory in Europe. The Yacht Club appears very tatty here, which must have also acted like a camouflage. More important priorities made such niceties as painting wait until after the war had ended.

London Road North, *c*. 1946. Many buildings on the left still show signs of shell damage. A Corporation bus passes the site of those shops destroyed in the Waller raid of 1942. On that side of the road there are bomb sites as far as the eye can see.

Sorting fish on the quayside, Waveney Dock, *c.* 1945. Life slowly returned to normal after the war, and in June 1945 LT 245 *JAP*, owned by W.H. Podd, was one of the first trawlers to land since the port's closure in 1940. Despite the five year respite all was not well, and a year later fishermen's strikes were spreading along the East Coast.

Fireman Jimmy Burwood at the Playhouse fire, 7 June 1946. The Phoenix Players were presenting *Blithe Spirit* that week and the troupe lost all their costumes and props. Playing to full houses, they concluded their week using the Sparrow's Nest Theatre as a temporary venue. *The Sacred Flame* had been planned for the coming week!

The old coach house with 91 London Road North on the corner of the Prairie, *c.* 1945. The final view of the old studio from the Prairie sees it wrecked by shrapnel and bomb blast, gutted by fire, and with much of its roof gone. The building now looked quite forlorn. Across the way, what had once been Boots and the Fifty Shilling Tailors was now a cleared bomb-site. It would be some while before reconstruction would begin. Because of the fire, Wilson was unable to get compensation for the damage suffered in the Waller raid. Before the war both shops were highly desirable properties; now, however, the pair were eventually sold for £2,000 to a Norwich consortium for redevelopment. Paige's and Bata Shoes were there from the 1950s to the 1980s, when both shops were taken over by Dorothy Perkins. The Prairie is now part of the Britten Centre.

Christopher Wilson retired as a professional photographer in 1944, although he continued to record the town in its early postwar years. The boarding house in Marine Parade was sold in 1947, and he then moved back to the Prairie to relive old memories. In 1950, after a short spell with Muriel, he decided to live with his favourite daughter, Joan, and moved with the family when they went down to Ipswich in 1952, where he died on 26 November 1953 at the age of eighty-one. He was buried beside his beloved Agnes in St Margaret's church, Lowestoft.

5
Oulton Broad

The path by Leathes Ham, *c.* 1912. This is an ancient and picturesque route at the foot of Normanston Park, then the home of Arthur Monckton, linking Lowestoft with Oulton Broad. Cut off from Lake Lothing with the arrival of the railway, it has become the home of much wildlife.

The Wherry Hotel and Mutford Bridge and lock, 1894, just before the replacement of the old 1820s bridge and lock gates. This is one of the earliest views of Oulton Broad taken by Christopher Wilson for Boughton, and looks across to the Oulton side; the bridge over the lock linked Oulton and Carlton Colville parishes together. George Mason, the proprietor of the homely Wherry Inn shown here centre left, was soon to replace it with a larger, grandiose structure. The centre of activities on the Broad, the old inn, like the Suffolk Hotel in Lowestoft before it, was quickly outgrowing its size. It was frequented by authors and painters alike: George Borrow was a regular here, as was the Broads writer Ernest Suffling, who also left a short description of the inn's interior, of which the bar-parlour in particular was considered 'quite a museum' with relics and curios from all over the world, including a locally caught stuffed and mounted otter. The inn also proudly described itself as the headquarters of London fishermen, and was only five minutes away from Oulton Broad station (now Oulton Broad North). A hundred years later many of the buildings seen opposite on the right would be demolished when the present bridge was constructed in the early 1990s.

Oulton Broad, mid-1890s. Approximately 1½ miles west of Lowestoft, with the arrival of the railway it became a veritable gentlemen's paradise, renowned for its yachting and its fishing. Here, craft catering for parties as large as twelve people are being made ready for hiring either by the day or half-day. Two boats moored near the opposite shore seem to be converted North Shields smacks. Perch, pike, roach and bream attracted many down from London, and with the cut between the Broad and the River Waveney, wherrymen soon found a new source of income hiring themselves and their boats out for the season. This early view by the young Christopher Wilson shows that he seems to have taken naturally to the beauty of the Broads, as they possibly reminded him of his birthplace, Sleaford, with its own opportunities of fishing and boating, and where as a young boy he learnt to swim and to catch fish barehanded. Much of this chapter, therefore, has a personal feel. For much of his life in Lowestoft, Oulton Broad and the countryside around attracted him and eventually, in 1917, the family rented, and later owned, their own little part of the Broads near Sadler's Creek.

The Wilson family houseboat on Oulton Broad, *c.* 1921. Moored at Sadler's Creek, with Swonnell's maltings on the Park Estate in the background, this particular boat was built before the First World War and could be converted into two cabins which could accommodate six people. Victor Wilson stands on the roof, while Bert Sterry holds an infant Joan. Agnes is sitting on the veranda. The success of the studio during the First World War enabled the family to rent a small bungalow nearby, which, with their houseboat not far away, enabled Christopher to pursue his hobby of fishing in all weathers. Never designed for travelling far, these houseboats were moved like punts. They had to be treated with respect, however, as Muriel's fiancé, 'Jock' Anderson, found out after trying to get from the stern to the bow via the small step seen here underneath the cabin windows, and promptly falling in the Broad.

St Michael's church, Oulton, *c.* 1906. Originally built in the shape of a crucifix and dating back to the fifteenth century, the church had at one time belonged to the Fastolf family. Apart from the tower, the building has changed little over the intervening years. This is very much a family photograph: Agnes and young Victor are looking towards St Michael's while little Muriel stands next to a tall headstone.

The Wilsons' house on the corner of Caldecott Road, early 1920s. Designed for the family by a local architect, H. Steward Watling, it was built mainly for the seasonal trade. The large windows seen here offered spectacular views across the Broads. However, problems with the builders meant that the project was a financial disaster.

'Mr Meakin's Bungalow', 1920s. This was actually Sylhet Bungalow on the Park Estate on the Oulton side of the Broad, and the home of Malcolm McMeekin. With a view looking across to the Everitt estate on the opposite shore and on towards Carlton Colville, the bungalow was situated in what was to become Caldecott Road, and shows the reason why living near the Broads was so popular.

The Wilson family at Fisher's Row near Oulton, c. 1927, situated between Oulton Dyke and the cut linking the Broad to the River Waveney. Victor's fiancée, Dorothy, looks on while Victor himself and Agnes sit in the boat after a gentle row from Oulton Broad. Joan, like her father, took eagerly to water and stands ankle-deep in the Broad. A good spot for a picnic, it was also an ideal place for fishing.

The Wilsons and Jenkins on the ice at Oulton Broad, February 1929. For a few days in mid-February the Broad froze over, and for the first time since 1895 skating matches were held. Hundreds arrived on the Friday to take part, including the younger adults of both the Jenkins and the Wilson families. With them was the young Joan Wilson, seen here bending over to check her skates.

Margaret Jenkins on the ice, Oulton Broad, February 1929. The ice lasted for around a week, much to everyone's enjoyment – although I would have thought that having to sit on it to secure your skates must have been a bit uncomfortable, to say the least. The ice held well enough for skating to continue until the following Thursday.

Katja, built by J.W. Brooke for Mawdesley Brooke in 1932, and photographed in the same year on the Broads. She was 49 ft in length and constructed of teak, pine and English oak, and cost over £1,200 to build. A similar vessel was constructed for Howard Hollingsworth of Bourne and Hollingsworth, London.

On the Broads, 1938. 'Lowestoft for Health and Frank Rice for Pleasure Boats' says the banner on this boat seen not far from the Wherry Hotel. Established in about 1937 and based at the Yacht Station next to Nicholas Everitt Park, Frank Rice appears to have survived for only a short period, ousted as many were, by the outbreak of war in 1939.

Robert Seth Stranack, posing here with his famed stopwatch and percussion-cap gun used to start many a yacht race, 1930s. He had lived at 'Breakspear' in Cotmer Road since 1908, and in the 1920s and 1930s became both a town councillor and also a county councillor. His immediate neighbour at one time was George Frederick Spashett.

A view towards Bridge Road, *c*. 1930. A man guards a bonfire on what had not long before been marshland. Looking across to Bridge Road is the tower of St Mark's. Once part of Carlton Colville and now the parish church of Oulton Broad, St Mark's was built in 1884 on a site given by George Edwards.

ACKNOWLEDGEMENTS

In the preparation of *Images of Lowestoft*, first and foremost I would like to acknowledge my deepest and sincerest gratitude to Mrs Joan Plant, the youngest child of Christopher Wilson, who not only introduced me to her father's work, but in sharing the story of his life, allowed me the privilege of using many of the photographs featured in this book, and introduced me to what is now almost a long-lost part of the town's history. It is no exaggeration to state that without her this book could never had been written. Secondly, I would like to acknowledge the help and encouragement that the Lowestoft branch of the Suffolk Record Office has given me over the years, in particular many thanks to Louis Clarke, David Wright, Bill Wexlar and Gudrun Reinke, who have all been kindness itself. I would also like to thank the Britten-Pears Library at Aldeburgh for their very kind permission in allowing me to use the portrait of the young Benjamin Britten on page 57. Many thanks also to friends and colleagues who have allowed me the use of the following photographs: Peter Killby (page 41); Ray Vincent – Studio 161 (pages 9, 26, 38 top); the late Jack Rose (pages 35, 40 bottom). The following are from my own archive; pages 2, 12, 13 (top), 16 (both), 33 (top), 37 (both), 42, 86 (bottom).

Thanks also to Jane Jarvis and her staff at the Lowestoft Heritage Workshop Centre, fellow members of the Jack Rose Old Lowestoft Society and to Sleaford Public Library for answering any queries that have arisen. Most of the notes on the Wilson family, notably on Christopher himself, have been adapted from my unpublished biography, *Christopher Wilson – the Forgotten Photographer of Lowestoft*.